CALIFORNIA
IN COLOR
The Paradox of Plenty

CALIFORNIA *in Color*

An Essay on

THE PARADOX OF PLENTY

and Descriptive Texts by

T. H. WATKINS

HASTINGS HOUSE · PUBLISHERS

New York

The text is dedicated to Joan,
who knows the reason why.

PUBLISHED 1970 BY HASTINGS HOUSE, PUBLISHERS, INC.

Published simultaneously in Canada by
Saunders, of Toronto, Ltd., Don Mills, Ontario

Library of Congress Catalog Card Number: 74-119795
SBN 8038-1140-3

Printed and bound in England by Jarrold and Sons Ltd., Norwich

CONTENTS

The Paradox of Plenty

PART ONE

AN ISLAND CALLED CALIFORNIA

I

CALIFORNIA is an island. More than 450 years ago, before Cortez crushed the Aztec empire of Montezuma, before Pizarro looted the kingdom of the Incas, a Spanish novelist said it all in a romance entitled *Las Sergas de Esplandin*: "Know ye that on the right hand of the Indies there is an island called California, very near the terrestrial paradise. . . ." García Rodríguez Ordoñez de Montalvo, the many-named novelist in question, could be forgiven his geographical ignorance; it would be nearly two centuries before the myth-ridden Spanish conquerors of the New World would learn that California did not hover mistily detached from the rest of North America. Besides, it did not matter, for California began as a mythic island and has remained a kind of mythic island even in an age that prides itself on the rejection of myth and the conquest of lateral space. We are no longer ignorant of geography; there are children today who know the whereabouts of the Isle of Wight, of Tierra del Fuego, of Hudson's Bay—and even some who can describe the outlines of Viet Nam. The world has become an Educational Toy, and only in the blank mysteries of vertical space do we find the shimmering explorer's myths so necessary to the footling soul of man. Yet California is still a repository of dreams that border on myth and a land in spiritual remove from the continent, an island on the western edge of a sea of land. This peculiarity is necessary to an understanding of this most American of all the American states. She is, as Carey McWilliams, one of her critics and admirers, has called her, the "great exception", and if her exceptional pathology can be attributed to any one factor, it is that her development has been the development of a region in isolation.

The geography of the state has been the most obvious factor in her isolation, of course, and until the building of the transcontinental railroad in 1869, that physiology made her nearly as remote and difficult to get to as a Himalayan Shangri-La. In the southeast portion of the state lie the dead reaches of the Mojave and Colorado deserts, formidable obstacles in the days of pre-automobile travel; north of that, the eastern approach is blocked by the long gray walls of the Sierra Nevada, one of the great mountain ranges in America and until the age of the freeway one of the most difficult to cross. The far north of the state is cut off from the Pacific Northwest by the tangled Klamath-Siskiyou Range. South of her is Mexico's Baja California, a peninsula whose desert mountains and jumbled topography are even today largely inaccessible by anything less than a Land Rover, and to the west there is nothing but the great Pacific ocean, to which the state presents one of the longest and most treacherous coastlines in the world, with only three natural harbors worth mentioning—Humboldt, San Francisco, and San Diego bays. California's geography, then, has conspired to preserve myths, for when a traveller had crossed the deserts of the Southwest to La Ciudad de los Angeles, when he had struggled painfully over the passes of the Sierra Nevada and seen before him the rich yellow plains of the Sacramento Valley, when he had endured three to five months of ocean travel from the eastern coast of America and entered finally the Golden Gate, the only emotional response possible had to be one of exaggerated possibilities, a conviction that he had found indeed the land of milk and honey, the new American Eden. That this Eden too often fell short of expectations was never enough to kill the shining dream. It is much the same today, even for emigrants zipping across Donner Pass or through the Mojave Desert at seventy miles an hour from the East, the South or the Midwest—they still come anticipating a land where hopes become reality, a different land, a new land, and the stunningly dramatic face of the state provides a reinforcement of their vision. What else but a modified paradise could you expect from a state that possesses a Mount Whitney, the highest mountain in the continental United States outside Alaska, and a Death Valley, whose 279.6 feet below sea level is the lowest point in the country—each of which is but sixty miles from the other?

One more, less obvious physical factor has contributed to the state's real and imagined isolation from the rest of the country. Her diverse geography harbors a wealth of resources that have contributed to her financial independence throughout the history of American possession, a self-sufficiency that enabled her to forge an empire on the Pacific Coast that in little more than a quarter of a century was an effective rival to the venerable financial capitals of the East. Gold was the beginning, of course, gold in quantities unheard of on the American continent, enough gold to produce one of the largest mass migrations in human history, enough to make California a state less than two years after the end of the Mexican War, and enough to make her a power in the halls of Congress when the bulk of the trans-Mississippi West was but little removed from *terra incognita*. But gold was not all. She was rich in timber; great stands of redwood trees (*Sequoia sempervirens*) forested the coastal ranges from the Klamath River in the north to the Santa Lucia Mountains in the south, and white pine and sugar pine covered the western slopes of the Sierra Nevada. She was rich in soil, so much so that the great farms of the Central Valley in the 1880s supplied much of the western world with wheat and presaged the time when California would become, as it is today, the most productive agricultural state in the nation, an agriculture fortified by a diversity

8

of climate and topography that allows almost anything indigenous to any region of the world to be grown somewhere within the state—from artichokes and avocados to rice and tangerines. And she was rich in oil, a resource that generally lay dormant and untapped until the age of the automobile, then exploded forth into one of the most stupendous industries in the West, and one that remains today a major force in the economics of the nation. Yellow gold, green gold, and black gold—these forces helped the state maintain itself as a largely independent unit in the past, and while her economic ties to the rest of the nation are today enormously complex and entangling (particularly in the area of government defense and aerospace contracts), that century-old thread of self-sufficiency was a major factor in the formation of her emotional life.

California has been a land populated by seekers, by men who came, and continue to come, for a new beginning, wanderers cut off from the roots of their many cultures. Her social evolution, then, has been freewheeling and experimental, far more sensitive to internal compulsions than to those of the world outside her land- and sea-locked boundaries. The description is perhaps simplistic; California has been settled by men, and men do not function entirely independent of their backgrounds. Yet it can serve to point up the fact that California has been throughout her history a stage on which men's dreams and aspirations have been turned loose to play out their roles generally unhampered by the restrictions of precedent and dogma. The result—as in a biological culture devoted to the production of new antibodies—has been the fermentation of a social environment of incredible variety and often startling peculiarities. It is no accident, after all, that one of the governors of this most populous state in the nation has been Ronald Reagan, a man who spent the bulk of his adult life engaged in the manufacture of celluloid dreams.

2

In the more than three centuries between 1542, when Jaõa Rodriguez Cabrilho, a Portuguese explorer in the employ of Spain, discovered San Diego Bay for Spain, and 1848, when the United States assumed title from Mexico, California drifted in a kind of historical vacuum, far behind the monumental changes of the world and the continent. For two centuries, in fact, Spain did next to nothing about her new possession. In the first place, after her first glory years of empire in the New World her power, steadily undermined by over extension and a lack of money, deteriorated to the point where she was struggling simply to survive against the growing strength of England and France; she had little energy left for colonizing efforts, much less actual development. Secondly the region was an unknown factor. The face of California presented to the sea-faring explorer was an obscure one, marked by coastal ranges that masked the interior and by few harbors fit to inspire total confidence (San Francisco Bay, for example, was not even discovered until 1769); moreover, the few natives that the explorers encountered between 1542 and 1769 had not displayed a tractable nature. In short, the effort and money involved in settling and developing the area was not justified by any visible potential. It was not until the other European powers, chiefly Russia, began to show some interest in California in the middle of the eighteenth century that Spain, insecure and somewhat desperate, decided that she had better make the region an outpost of empire to serve as a buffer against foreign intrusion.

In 1769, Gaspar de Portolá and Fray Junípero Serra set out with a colonizing party from the northern part of Baja California. At the site of San Diego, Serra established the first mission in California, and Portolá, after one unsuccessful attempt, made his way the following year to Monterey Bay, where he founded a presidio and the mission of San Carlos. In 1776, Juan Bautista de Anza led a major colonizing party of 240 men, women, and children across the Colorado and Mojave deserts from Sonora to San Gabriel, then north to Monterey, and finally to San Francisco Bay, where he selected sites for a presidio and a mission. This last expedition, to all intents, was the final major effort made by Spain to colonize the island called California. Between 1769 and 1822, the year that Mexico successfully established her independence from Spain, the Mother Country left a record of settlement that was anemic by any standards, and certainly by the standards of her more glorious past: twenty missions, three presidios (military establishments), two pueblos (civil towns), and a population of missionaries, settlers, and soldiers of about thirty-seven hundred. It was all a far cry from the days when the ruthless legions of the *conquistadores* had planted the cross of empire on the shores of the New World.

Mexico herself did little better. The land approach to California from Sonora, opened by Anza in 1776, was closed in 1781, when the previously friendly Yuma Indians became contentious, and remained an unreliable communications link with the government in· Mexico throughout the period of her rule. The only remaining connection was by sea, a tenuous, time-consuming, and often dangerous approach. California was generally left to her own devices, and evolved a culture peculiarly suited to her time and place: a pastoral society dependent upon husbandry and the kind of subsistence agriculture practiced by the missions. When the great expanses of mission lands were taken over by the government in 1833 and passed on to private ownership, it simply expanded the phenomenon, which some historians have maintained was one of the greatest non-nomadic pastoral societies in human history. California, it might be said, had been converted into an immense pasture, at least as indicated by the state's most prolific historian, Hubert Howe Bancroft: "A Californian never used to speak of his farm by acres, but by leagues. One of four or five leagues was considered quite small. A thrifty farmer should have 2,000 horses, 15,000 head of cattle, and 20,000 sheep, as his productive stock, on which he should not encroach, except in an emergency." A typical pre-American rancho was that of Mariano Vallejo, north of San Francisco; it comprised thirty-three leagues—or 146,000 acres—of which all but 500 acres were given over to grazing land. Simple, pleasure-looking, and casual to the point of indolence, it was a society that existed in a backwash of time, and would prove to be no match for the vigor and exploitive enterprise of the industrial age brought to the golden shores of California by hordes of Yankees.

In 1846, the United States went to war with Mexico for the specific purpose of territorial expansion (the only such war in her history, with the possible exception of the Spanish–American "War" of 1898). Two years, $100,000,000, and 12,000 American lives later, she acquired enough territory to nearly double her physical size. Included was California, a land much less known or understood by most Americans in 1848 than, say, Viet Nam is today. Nevertheless, some Americans not only had heard of California, but had picked up and moved there, some as traders, others as settlers seeking a portion of agricultural land whose richness had been luring American settlers since the early 1840s. By 1848, there were about 2,000 foreigners, mostly American, residing in California out of a total non-Indian population of approximately 12,000. While American acquisition certainly assured a steady period of regular growth, similar to that already taking place in Oregon to the north, it does not seem likely that under normal circumstances there would have been such an immediate and profound shift in the region's patterns of development that it would be lifted from the pastoral age to the industrial age in less than two years.

The difference was gold. The importance of the discovery of gold to California's American life cannot possibly be overstated. It was the single most traumatic experience in the state's history; it laid the foundation for a new citadel of power on the Pacific Coast; its madness infected all of American life, in one way or another, and its legacy of hysteria, exploding population, boom-and-bust psychology, transience, and cosmopolitanism has played a significant and continuing role in the formation of the state's emotional pathology.

There were two Gold Rushes, the first in early 1848. Gold had been discovered in January on the American River, and by March there were enough miners in the area to make gold an "article of traffic", so the *California Star* reported, at Captain John Sutter's New Helvetia, the site of the future Sacramento. Still, it was a generally quiet affair until May, when Sam Brannan, an entrepreneur who had a general store going up near the diggings and knew a good thing when he saw it, came riding into San Francisco waving a bottle of nuggets over his head and shouting, "Gold! Gold on the American River!" Why this sudden announcement should have electrified the town— which had heard of the gold long before this—is a curiosity left unanswered by history. Nevertheless, there is no question about its effect, which bordered on the grotesque. The embryonic little cities of San Francisco and Monterey all but emptied. Merchants deserted their shops, crews their ships, and captains their crews—and all headed for the diggings, equipped with whatever seemed useful for getting at the gold. By July, there were more than 3,000 miners scrambling over the lands in and about the Sierra foothills. By the end of the year, they were joined by nearly 10,000 Mexicans and Chileans, the first outsiders to get word of the discovery. During the course of the year, the enterprising firstcomers extracted at least six million dollars worth of gold, more than enough to justify the astonishment of none other than President James K. Polk, reflected in his December State of the Union message to Congress: "The accounts of the abundance of gold in that territory are of such an extraordinary character as would scarcely command belief, were they not corroborated by the authentic reports of officers in the public service. . . ."

Duty called, and America responded. There was gold to be had, more gold than the legions of Coronado might have dreamed of, more gold than the American experience had prepared her citizens to even think about. Thousands streamed into the eastern ports, willing and ready to board any available vessel bound for California. Between mid-December, 1848, and mid-January, 1849, 61 ships with an average of fifty passengers each sailed for California from New York, Boston, Salem, Philadelphia, Baltimore, and Norfolk. Ships in ports all over the world cancelled their commitments and sailed for the east coast of America, eager to grab off their share of the passenger explosion, and by the end of 1849 more than 600 of them had sailed through the Golden Gate, carrying at least 45,000 new arrivals.

Another 45,000 came by land in 1849 across trails that were so crowded they resembled highways. These were not lonely, trailbreaking pioneers, but the 2,000-mile trip did possess its hazards—among them accidental shootings, drownings, and cholera picked up in the disease-ridden valley of the Mississippi. It was a migration of amateurs, rank greenhorns in the techniques of the westward movement. However, they *were* pioneers in the establishment of one of America's more slovenly traditions: the fouling of the western environment. Most of the trails from St. Joseph, Independence, and Council Bluffs converged at one point or another on the Platte River, and this shallow, helpless stream was transformed into an enormous sewer whose water quickly became unfit to drink. They littered, too, abandoning broken-down wagons, useless equipment, excess baggage, and enough spoiled and superfluous food, including great stacks of rancid bacon slabs, that a blind man might have been able to get to California with nothing but the stench to show him the way.

Whether by land or by sea, the men who came were a curious lot in the annals of American pioneering. They were not settlers, but gamblers with one obsession: to strike it rich in California and return to their homes in the East with a stake to take them through the rest of life in ease and luxury. The dream was very nearly a moral imperative; in the eyes of most of them, it would have been a crime against themselves, their families, and their futures to have ignored the lorelei of gold. They came from all walks of life—and from most of the major countries of the western world—and were young, most of them in their twenties, and a startling number in their teens. Most of them came from solid, if not affluent backgrounds; after all, it took money, quite a bit of money for the time, to get to California. It was an investment in the future, an act of faith similar to that of today's suburbanite, who buys stock on margin and hocks himself to the teeth in the anticipation of rewards to come. The great bulk of them were not only literate, but downright literary; superbly self-conscious of the fact that they were taking part in a movement of great historic import, they left behind an enormous collection of diaries, journals, letters, and reminiscences, making the Gold Rush one of the most thoroughly documented experiences in national history. The picture of these young, vigorous, womanless, exploitive amateurs scribbling away for the sake of posterity is far removed from that stereotyped image of the western pioneer we have come to know, and perhaps love: the grimjawed and ruggedly determined settler who, with his patient, durable wife and towheaded children, trundled his worldly possessions to a new beginning in the West, allowing neither sleet, snow, locusts, nor marauding bands of Comanches to deny him his God-given right to 160 sunbaked acres. The gold-seekers couldn't have cared less about acreage—unless it happened to possess gold loose enough to be picked up, in Mark Twain's phrase, "with a long-handled shovel".

For California, the Gold Rush was an enormous success story. Before 1849, her population had been a little over 12,000; by 1852, generally considered to be the year that the Rush officially ended, that figure had been bloated to more than 220,000. In that same three-year period, a province whose most profitable enterprise had once been the production of hides and tallow produced an estimated $214,000,000 worth of gold —more than twice the cost of the Mexican War. In less than two years, San Francisco was transformed from a soporific little port town to the largest city west of Chicago, complete with banks, industries, hotels, restaurants, brothels, innumerable taverns, a solidly-entrenched criminal class, political chicanery, and all the other paraphernalia common to mid-nineteenth century urban life; and in 1850, California became a full-fledged American state, with an allotment of Congressmen and Senators, and an influence in the windswept caverns of Capitol Hill that no western state would ever hope to match.

For innumerable of its participants, however, the Gold Rush was little short of personal tragedy, a paradox hinted at powerfully in an agonized letter of 1852 from one Ananias Rogers: "I am solitary & alone. Am I never to see my loved ones again? If I had determined to make a permanent residence in this valley [the Sacramento] I might now have been well off, but my whole anxiety was to make a sudden raise and return to my family. This I undertook to do by mining. This is certainly the most uncertain of any business in the world. . . . Indeed I do not know what to do. Oh that I could once more be with my family. Alas, I fear this never may be. Oh me, I am weak in body & I fear worse in mind. . . ."

No one knows what happened to Ananias Rogers. It may be that he did make it back to his family in the East. If so, he returned, like thousands of others (23,000 in 1852 alone), broken in spirit and perhaps in body. They had arrived in California young; most of them returned, like men from the agonies of war, aged by their experience, sobered and possibly matured by the follies of greed that had led them West. Few of them ever forgot this period of their lives, and in later years many of them, stricken by the knowledge that they had participated in history, set down their memories of that experience in reminiscences, stories in which the struggle to survive, the privation, the hunger, the frustration, and the failure were softened in the glow of recollection. But none, it is safe to say, returned from California with the same confidence in the reality of dreams. The reason for their failure was simple: there just was not enough gold to go around. After the first year of mining, most of the loose surface gold, which could profitably be extracted by one or two men with the simplest of equipment and effort, was depleted by the thousands who had scrambled over the Sierra foothills like so many beetles on a corpse in 1848 and early 1849. The bulk of the remaining gold—and there was a great deal of it—was at the bottom of rivers whose courses had to be changed to make it available, imbedded in hills that had to be washed away with powerful streams of water, or locked in quartz veins deep in the earth, where only mining and milling could get it out—all processes that required a considerable capital investment, sophisticated technology, and an extensive labor force. The American Everyman had none of these, and so thousands who did not return East found themselves suddenly part of the laboring classes, working for mining companies whose owners resided in the red plush atmosphere of monopoly, as itinerant laborers for farmers who had staked out sweeping vistas of farmland in the coastal and interior valleys, or for city merchants who had been canny enough to realize that there was more gold to be found in the gold seekers than in the Sierran hills. Some, like Jasons blinded by their own hopes, continued to wander the pockets and crannies of the West for years, refusing to relinquish the dream and in their "prospecting" giving birth to a name and a tradition. Others—we will never know how many—were driven to suicide or to the slow death of alcoholism and the netherworld of the half-life.

This is a dismal picture, certainly, and hardly representative of the larger narrative of California's early American life. Yet it is a picture that too often has been obscured by the electric excitement of the Gold Rush and the tremendous growth that it inspired. Moreover, it is a picture that may provide a deeper understanding of a state whose one prevailing theme through the years has been the paradox of excess: incredible wealth existing side-by-side with poverty beyond belief, revolutionary political and social progress with oppression and intolerance of fascistic dimensions, pride in a burgeoning population with a despair of ever learning to control it, and the glow of rising expectations with the misery of ruined hopes.

3

I have gone on at such length about the California Gold Rush because there is very little in the course of the state's history that cannot be linked, one way or another, to the patterns of life and growth exhibited by that grand catharsis. What California has become is largely the result of a series of stupendous economic, political, and social detonations of which the Gold Rush was not merely the first, but was the prime mover —the beginning of a chain reaction whose end is yet to come. Even the most piecemeal discussion of the post-Gold Rush history of the state is a lesson in the dynamics of cultural explosion, and in spite of the complexity of her history and a spontaneity of change that often smacks of anarchy, her evolution has been typified by the continuation of a few major themes for more than a century.

The key to that evolution has been population growth. It is one of the axioms of California history that her population has doubled every twenty years since 1850, the most dramatic manifestation of regional growth in the nation; her annual population increase of 3.8 per cent has remained consistently higher than that of the country at large, often double the national rate. While no period has ever matched the proportional increase of that between 1848 and 1852—when the population grew by almost two thousand per cent—there have always been long periods during which the state's growth took on the proportions of boom similar to that of the Gold Rush years. The Southern California land boom of the 1880s, the exodus out of the Midwest in the 1920s, the migration of misery out of the great Dust Bowl of the 1930s, the incredible rush for jobs during the years of World War II, and the postwar boom of a suddenly affluent and eminently mobile society—all these have been in the tradition established by the Gold Rush and have contributed mightily to the state's present condition as the most populous in the nation, with more than twenty million people within its boundaries. An even more startling statistic is the rate of growth in Southern California since 1900, which illustrates the one major dynamic in California's twentieth-century history: the quicksilver shift of power to the south. Between 1900 and the present, Los Angeles has grown like a hypertropic mushroom, more than 3,000 per cent, while San Francisco has limped along at a rate well under 150 per cent, and in recent years actually has shown signs of falling off. A combination of factors has conspired to produce the dominance of Los Angeles in the population sweepstakes—not the least of which is the simple geographical fact that she has more room to grow than San Francisco. A superior climate, the incredible Lorelei of Hollywood that has given all of Southern California an air of synthetic glamor, probably unmatched on the continent, and the postwar boom in heavy industry—these and more have gone into the creation of the extruded metropolis south of the Tehachapis. Today, more than 11,000,000 people reside in Southern California, and if it is true, as many are maintaining, that California represents the new America, then by sheer weight of numbers the megalopolis of Southern California must represent the new California, a prospect that has given some observers the galloping fantods.

Equally significant has been the kind and quality of the state's population increase and this, even more than the increase itself, represents the consistency of tradition. Since 1850, the bulk of the population growth has been the result of immigration, in recent years holding an average ratio over natural increase by sixty-to-forty, and in many previous years far exceeding that ratio (between 1920 and 1930, for example, of the added population of 2,500,000 less than 250,000 had been born in the state). This unique factor in the state's growth patterns has had measurable effect on just about every aspect of her economic, political, and social life and has given birth to an organization styling itself the Native Sons and Daughters of the Golden West, whose rationale seems to be that there is something peculiarly distinctive, perhaps superior, about a person born in California, as opposed to someone whose only claim to good sense was that he recognized the rather obvious delights that waited on the western edge of the continent. Then again, the organization may represent nothing more complicated than the typically paranoid reaction of a resident minority which finds itself surrounded by hordes of outsiders—outsiders that have comprised as much as 76 per cent of the total population.

Not only mobile in the sense that it has moved to California from points east, that population has displayed in the past and continues to display an astonishing mobility *within* the state. Californians have been described as a rootless breed, and not without justification; they tend to move about with the apparent aimlessness of particles in liquid suspension. This curious syndrome is a statewide phenomenon, but also takes place within localities. In Southern California, for example, one out of every three families changes houses once a year. (One of the agonies that is afflicting a Post Office Department that appears to be strangling is the simple chore of keeping up with such people.) It must be assumed that the majority of them are not necessarily skipping out on their creditors. Californians *like* to move; in a state in which the economic virtues assume canted, not to say distorted, characteristics, movement of this kind is considered a sign of social progress, not instability. To move, generally speaking, is to move up—up to a better job, up to a better house, up to a more genteel neighbourhood. Some, of course, must be moving down, but it is safe to say that the majority are jumping about in pursuit of bigger and better rainbows. Here, too, we find intriguing hints of the Gold Rush years, when men scurried from one golden pocket of opportunity to another and left as their most durable legacy a conviction that the grandest of all the great strikes was waiting over the next hogback ridge. Californians still are wanderers with the light of tomorrow in their eyes.

Another characteristic of this wandering population is its diversity. California, from the beginning of her history as an American state, has been an ethnic potpourri—a veritable bouillabaise of humanity. This is not to say that the state's variegated collection of humanity has always mixed well; in point of fact, variety has given birth to some of the more sordid escapades in her history, from the pogrom launched against the Chinese of Los Angeles in 1871 (22 killed) to the contorted agony of Watts in 1965 (30 killed). Nevertheless, diversity has colored the cultural weave of the state's population, giving vigor to her writing, her art, her life.

The first minority in the state's history, of course, were the resident owners, the Mexicans. After the inundation of the gold rush, California's Mexicans gradually retreated to little pockets of misery, and even today there is hardly a good-sized hamlet in the state that does not have its "Mexican Town", a shack and shanty equivalent of an eastern tenement district. Curiously, while overwhelming the Mexican's culture, the Anglo has been positively fascinated with its remnants. Millions of people annually trek to California's surviving missions to stare in hushed awe at these crumbling artifacts of an age past memory; local museums scattered over the countryside invariably feature aged paraphernalia—costumes, teacups, silverware, etc.—left over from the local manifestation of Spanish empire; misty romances, a startling number of them written by the proverbial Little Old Lady, have been inspired by California's pastoral period and have run like a silver thread through the state's literary history; and no parade or civic bachannalia would be complete without a living descendent from one of the local "Spanish" families, done up in the costume of the dons. (The quotation marks around "Spanish", incidentally, were placed there deliberately to point up the Anglo's peculiar determination to refer to Mexicans of his acquaintance as being of Spanish extraction, as if the nationalistic distinction made them somehow more "presentable". A Mexican lawyer of Los Angeles once responded to such a description of himself with considerable heat: "Spanish, hell! I'm an Aztec!")

Mexican–Americans are still the largest minority group in California—always excluding members of the Native Sons and Daughters—but the past century and more has brought them a great deal of company. The Chinese, brought first by the lure of gold and later imported in droves by railroad builders and the labor-hungry farmers of the interior valleys, eventually gravitated to the cities—Los Angeles and San Francisco in particular—and there congregated in "Chinatowns" whose picturesque squalor have made them money-making tourist attractions for nearly a century. Occasionally, some spoilsport calls them ghettoes, but not often enough to seriously impair their usefulness as chamber of commerce brochure items. The Chinese were followed by the Japanese, who came to work on the farms of California for wages, although many thousands had the ill grace to go to farming for themselves. After the Japanese came the Hindus, and after the Hindus the Filipinos—each in waves of migration inspired by the farmer's continuing need for a large, transient labor force willing to work for wages the farmers were willing to pay. In such a way, California managed to import the great bulk of her minorities. Even native Americans have been "imported" to the state. During the agonizing Dust Bowl years "Okies" and "Arkies" flocked to California, following the hope of decent wages on California farms (a vision which, as usual, did not quite come true for most of them) and during World War II thousands of Negroes from the American South flocked to fill the jobs created by rapidly expanding industrial complexes on the Pacific Coast, an immigration that has not ceased even today, when most of these job-seeking Negroes find themselves banked up on the western edge of the continent with no place to go. California still boasts the golden dream, but for some the dream has withered, as it did for so many of the goldseekers more than a century ago.

The result of all this immigration has created an incredible hodge-podge of peoples in this island called California, probably—with the admitted exception of portions of the East Coast—the most widely various assembly of life-styles on the continent, from the American Indian huddled in a hovel in the San Francisco Bay Area and dreaming of his people's past to an electronics engineer barbecueing spare ribs in the serene middle-class elegance of his Anaheim split-level; from the rancorous Black Power advocate of Oakland to the smugly isolated dowager of Beverley Hills; from the rock artist of the Sunset Strip to the primadonna of the San Francisco Opera. California is a human crazy-quilt, with all of the virtues and most of the agonies of mainstream America—and a few of both unique to herself.

Her history has been a great exaggeration dominated by the gold rush and punctuated by periodic expressions of insanity similar to that grand excitement—all of it a history produced by a shifting, drifting, ever-seeking population whose needs and wants have not only changed from generation to generation but often from year to year and even week to week. Consider, for a moment, her politics. "The politics of California", James Bryce said in *The American Commonwealth* (1889), "is unique". He was exercising the British privilege of understatement, as the following examination of a few selected incidents in California's political history might indicate. In 1849 a statewide election was held to determine whether California should enter the union of the United States; less than 12,000 of the more than 100,000 qualified voters even bothered to show up at the polls, for the goldseekers could not have cared less—all they wanted to do was make their piles and return to the East. Two years later, San Francisco's citizens suddenly became so interested in the political condition of the city (which, to all intents and purposes, meant the political condition of the state) that they formed a Vigilance Committee and proceeded to clean the city up, more or less. In 1879 it was decided to work up a new state constitution, and the clamoring factions that made up the state's political anatomy at that time—ranging from "bosses" controlled by the Southern Pacific Railroad to the Workingman's Party, which wanted to boot the Chinese out of California—managed to contrive one of the most unworkable documents in American political history. California's constitution has been amended more than three hundred times since its adoption in 1879, each amendment seeking to satisfy one more of hundreds upon hundreds of special-interest factions in her confused political history. In 1911 Los Angeles, for years the citadel of unenlightened conservatism, came as close to electing a socialist mayor as it ever would in its history; this was in 1911, remember —a time when most of America considered socialism a disease hardly less pernicious than galloping cholera. In 1934 the entire *state* came within 300,000 votes of electing Upton Sinclair governor under the standard of EPIC (End Poverty in California), a program whose solutions to the disaster of the depression gave the "socialistic" legislation of Franklin Roosevelt the revolutionary appearance of resolutions passed by a local garden club. Continuing her maverick traditions, in 1964 the state overwhelmingly supported liberal Democrat Lyndon B. Johnson for president against an ultra-conservative while rejecting with equal force liberal Democrat Pierre Salinger for senator—in *favor* of an ultra-conservative. And as a final fillip to the curiosities of her political life, the state has seen fit to elect motion-picture actors to two of the most prestigious and demanding public offices in the country. There are sundry reasons for California's wayward political behavior over the past 120 years, but one of the most significant has got to be the fact that the caterwauling demands of her floating, exploding population have had all the consistency and predictability of a crap game with unloaded dice.

What is in store in the future for this "big, wayward girl", the state of California? If the past is indeed prologue, then her past is one of the least enlightening prologues in history, for it provides few guidelines from which to make confident predictions. Given the prologue of the past, it might be easy enough to say that she will continue to exhibit the explosive population growth of the last century, if it were not for the fact that simple arithmetic says that it can't be done. California's population has grown at a rate more than twice that of the country at large, as noted earlier: if it continues at that rate for the next century or so, as demographer Daniel P. Luten has pointed out, there will be about a billion people living in the state of California and about a billion living in the United States—in other words, everyone in the United States will live in California. If this strange phenomenon is not to occur, then the century-old patterns of immigration to California must stop; the seekers and the wanderers will have to go elsewhere in search of the golden dream. Given the prologue of the past, it seems reasonable to predict that the crowded, smog-ridden, uncontrolled megalopolis south of the Tehachapi Mountains is the outline of California's future; but who is to say that Californians will not achieve enlightenment, will not somehow take hold of their agonizing urban problems and with a technology that already is the wonder of the world re-create an environment fit for human habitation, and not simply follow the ruinous patterns of the past? Given the prologue of the past, it is safe to say that California's political and social life will continue to display maverick qualities, but no man could say with any degree of certainty where it will lead her next—down the path of righteousness or the road to hell.

Wherever she goes and whatever she does, it *is* reasonable to expect that she will perform with gusto, originality, and vigor; there has never been a region on earth quite like her, nor is there ever likely to be. She has been a stage on which tremendous fantasies have been performed; her excitement has been the excitement of the sudden, explosive present and the unknown future; her life has been the life of the gambler incapable of leaving the game, unwilling to account for tomorrow, and convinced that the next toss of dice will come up high, hard, and strong.

And to make predictions about the state of California is an exercise for fools.

PART TWO

O PANTHER OF THE SPLENDID HIDE...

I

IT IS QUITE impossible to love California in the way in which Pennsylvanians, Alabamans, and—most assuredly—Texans may be said to love their states. I say this as a member of California's largest minority group—the native-born son—and as a man who has not remained outside the state for longer than two weeks. At one time or another, I have become at least transiently familiar with much of her 158,000 square miles, from the desert wastelands of the south to the tangled green forests of the north, from the Sierras of the east to the Pacific of the west. I lived for twenty-four years in Southern California and have spent the last nine years in Northern California. As a writer, I have gleaned the details of her past to provide me with the raw material by which I make a living; as a devout conservationist, I have periodically polemicized against any alteration of her beauties; and as a sometime student of dramatic humor I have delved into her present politics, sociology, and, with marginal understanding, her technology. I would not willingly live anywhere else on earth.

My credentials would seem to qualify me as a man who could love California, but I cannot, and I seriously doubt that any man could. She is too big, too wide, too spread out in sheer physical excess to be lovable, and her past and present provide few emotional hooks on which a man can hang his devotion. Besides, to say that you love something is to imply that you understand it, and the task of understanding California, as we have seen, is a chore only a little less burdensome than learning to understand the dynamics of the solar system—a lifelong enterprise. Yet, while it is impossible to love California as a whole, her very size and diversity have made it possible for a man to love a great many *parts* of California with something akin to real passion. This multiplicity of choices in the matter of love—a veritable harem, if one cares to think of it that way—can satisfy the tastes of almost anyone and doubtless is one of the reasons why California still holds the promise of answered dreams to those thousands who continue to cross her borders. Listen, for a moment, to Julie Andrews on the delights of Los Angeles, as quoted in the *National Geographic*, May 1966:

"The beauty of Los Angeles is what I would call 'pulse'—that wonderful steady beat of energy. You feel it in the early morning, when the sun is barely up, the air is cool and quiet, yet there is already a hint of excitement. Then you drive down into that busy life, and you can't help thinking—'It's going to be another wonderful day!' What more can anyone ask of a city?"

Some people, myself included, might care to lavish their love on some place other than Los Angeles, but Miss Andrews' reaction to the city illustrates the fact that there are many Californias—perhaps as many as there are Californians to love them. There are those for whom the Sierran meadows of Grass Valley represent what they mean when they say California; there are those to whom La Jolla means California, those to whom Crescent City means California, those to whom San Luis Obispo means California, and even those to whom Anaheim must mean California. And each of these people can lay claim to several additional Californias to love. No man's view of the state is likely to be identical, or even very similar, to the view of any other man. It would be well to keep this fact in mind as the narrative that follows is read, for it is a narrative severely limited by the scope of my own well-loved Californias; it is nothing more than one man's rendering of some part of a state whose physical complexities would boggle the electrodes of a computer—if any computer were ever foolish enough to essay a description of California.

2

Deserts, mountains, and valleys—the interior landscape of California presents as wide a variety of topographic extremes as any region on the face of the earth. Each of these extremes offers a selection of delights to suit the palate of almost anyone, whether he be a lover of the solitude of limitless open space or peculiarly fond of the great, crowded caverns of a forest, and each is served by a statelong chain of National Parks, National Monuments, and State Parks—the most extensive park system in the country and one in which California can justifiably take pride.

Her deserts, like so much of everything in the state, are immense in size and dramatic in impact. The Mojave Desert, the Colorado Desert, and Death Valley comprise a great triangular wasteland in the southeastern portion of the state from Mexico on the south to the Inyo Mountains on the north, from the Colorado River on the east to the San Bernardino Mountains on the west. This land was in some prehistoric age covered by a great inland sea, and it carries with it today the feel of primordial time. Great stretches of it remain untouched by the workings of man; there are relatively few roads or highways, and as you traverse it on those roads that do exist it is altogether too easy to imagine yourself lost and alone, helpless in the face of elements as basic to the nature of the earth as the processes of life and death. You wonder as you cross the Mohave from Needles to Barstow how it was that men and women and oxen, trudging from one mirage-ridden, nearly waterless end of this rocky, tumbling-down country to the other, could have survived, and you remember that some of them didn't. Yet even as you feel the bleak oppression of the flat, hard sky and the Biblical stretch of wilderness you recognize an incredible kind of beauty in it all. The air is alive with heat, and its clarity enlarges the powers of vision; you take delight in the fact that you can distinguish a rock not much larger than a man many miles before you come upon it. As you become accustomed to the clarity, you begin to realize that there is beauty and variety in rock, in terms of both shape and color, to such an extent that the land about you takes on the flat, muted look of an abstract painting done in pastels. In the morning and evening hours, as the sun rises and sets, it toys with colors and densities of shadow like some temperamental artist reaching for perfection, from red to blue to purple to black, and in those hours when the sun is gone completely the sky is a thick black sea populated by so many stars that when the moon is new it is quite possible to read by starlight alone. When the moon is full, the landscape is quite indescribable; it is a time when there is no time.

This is the kind of country that poet and story-teller Charles F. Lummis described as the "land of ineffable lights". Death Valley is something else again. Death Valley is the graveyard of the earth, a sawtooth and alkali wilderness where little more than the most primitive vegetation can take a living grip on the land, and where there are areas where nothing at all will grow. Situated in the highest northern angle of the desert triangle, 550 square miles of the valley floor are below sea level, and Bad Water, a tiny collection of bitter salt pools, is the lowest point on the North American continent at −279.6 feet of altitude. During the summer months, while the days are a shimmering blast of sun and the rocks radiate stored heat at night, Death Valley is one of the hottest places on the face of the earth, registering temperatures that can fry a man's mind. Death Valley is a reminder of how the earth began—and how it will end.

More gentle reminders of the nature and variety of time are California's mountain ranges, whose bisecting crescents lace up the northern two-thirds of the state like the drawstring of a purse, from the border of San Bernardino County to the Oregon state line, and from the Nevada state line to the Pacific Ocean. The south has its ranges, too —the San Bernardino and the San Gabriel, principally—and its impressive peaks— Mount Wilson, Mount San Bernardino, and the particularly awesome Mount San Jacinto, which looms up from the desert surrounding Palm Springs like a massive blue wall—but the truly great ranges and peaks belong to the north. They are as various in style as they are in size. The Coast Range undulates north from Santa Barbara to San Francisco Bay in long ridges worn down by weather and time; above San Francisco, it slowly spreads out to the Oregon State line in a mighty jumble of tangled green wilderness, abetted by a climate that provides in some areas an annual rainfall of eighty inches. In the north central section of the state, where the Cascade Range joins the Klamoth-Siskiyou, are two of her most ponderous mountains, both remnants of the age of volcanoes: Mount Shasta and Mount Lassen. Mount Shasta is the Old White Lady of the north, whose snow-covered flanks rise out of the plain of the Shasta Valley like a transplanted Fujiyama. "Lonely as God and white as a winter moon", poet

Joaquin Miller described her, in probably the best-turned line that wonderful old con man ever worked up. To the south of her is Mount Lassen, a 10,453-feet reminder of the earth's geologic past. Unlike Mount Shasta, however, Lassen has not seen fit to die completely. She last erupted in 1914, and for the next two years exploded some three hundred times, sending molten lava streaming into her canyons, blasting rocks into the surrounding countryside, and blanketing the air in a hot smother of volcanic ash. The residue from that violent time can still be seen throughout Lassen Volcanic National Park. She is not expected to erupt again for a while; neither is she considered quite dead.

South of Lassen begins the 350-mile sweep of the Sierra Nevada, John Muir's magnificent "range of light". The Sierras are thick with history, for they comprise California's Great Wall on the east, a wall that had to be breached by the scores of thousands of footsore immigrants of the mid-nineteenth century before the new American Eden could be attained. The travails of crossing this range have been written indelibly on the memory of the past; James Reddeford Walker, a mountain man who discovered a pass through it in the 1830s; John Charles Fremont's exploring expedition of 1842 making the first winter crossing; the Stevens-Murphy party hauling the first wagons over the summit of Truckee Pass in 1844; the Donner Party reaching the bitter edge of despair at Donner Lake in 1846; the armies of tiny Chinese who painstakingly carved a railroad's right-of-way through it in 1866, 1867, and 1868. It was in the Sierras, too, that men scrabbled after the main chance of gold, infesting every nook and cranny that could conveniently be reached and scattering so much litter in their wake that today there is a booming market in century-old picks and pans, knives and bottles —the detritus of a transient subculture dribbled over the landscape like so many beer cans and banana peels. That cathartic heritage is sleekly preserved today throughout the Mother Lode country, from Grass Valley to Angel's Camp and Columbia—one of the more delightful restored towns in the history of artifactual preservation—and together with the stunning variety of recreational delights—fishing, hunting, simple camping, hiking, skiing, mountain-climbing, and blowing a week's pay in the casinos of Lake Tahoe—have made the Sierras one of the most popular year-round resort areas on the face of the earth. And if the opportunity to wallow in sheer excess of beauty is wanted, the grandiose wonders of Yosemite, Kings Canyon, and Sequoia national parks should be enough to fill any man's pleasure.

Between the Coast Range and the Sierra Nevada lie California's two great valleys —the Sacramento Valley in the North and the San Joaquin Valley in the south. Superbly watered by the Sacramento and San Joaquin Rivers and such tributaries as the Feather, the Yuba, the American, the Stanislaus, and the Merced, the two valleys comprise one of the most productive agricultural regions in human history. Agriculture in this region has always been an industry of monumental proportions; the small, self-sufficient "family farm" of America's fond past has never been a significant factor here, for the rich land was systematically locked up in huge tracts—first by the Mexicans, then by Anglo farmers lucky enough to have arrived early, then by the Southern Pacific Railroad, which was granted immense sweeps of land as an impetus to railroad construction, and finally to speculators of one ilk or another. The result has been land monopoly on a scale rarely matched in American history; today, for example, over two-and-one-half million acres of the nearly four million acres under cultivation on the west side of the San Joaquin Valley are held in tracts of no less than one thousand acres, and of these nearly a million acres are owned by but five corporations. These are not fields, but factories, places for machines, for time-and-motion studies, for specilization and efficiency, and for working men whose labor probably provides all the emotional satisfaction of tightening bolts in an automobile assembly plant—all of it a far cry from the fine, Arcadian vision of the independent yeoman that has been so much a part of America's past. But these wide "factories in the field" produce an agriculture that is the envy of the world in its diversity and wealth.

Diversity and wealth—the phrase is one that must recur again and again in any discussion of the offerings of California's topography, even in so brief a one as this. There is enough to satisfy any man. As a final note, consider trees for a moment.

A tree is an easily-loved object. A friend of mine, a quite successful lawyer and in most respects a man who exhibits all the characteristics of a normal male, has one disconcerting habit: he hugs trees. He will step up to a tree quite solemnly, hug it, and give it a friendly pat on the backside. "Trees are alive, you know," he will explain in the tones of a reasonable man. "They need love just as much as we do."

I have never hugged a tree, being a reticent person by inclination, but I have loved a great many of them. I can think of no region on earth more likely to satisfy the appetites of an unashamed tree lover than California. Every botanical life-zone except the tropical is represented somewhere in the state, and this diversity has allowed the proliferation of an astonishing variety of trees—including several strains not indigenous to the state that have flourished after their importation, from the Eucalyptus to the Orange. In shape and physiognomy they vary from the dry, feathery-barked Joshua trees of the Southern California desert, with their strange spiked blooms and their curious resemblance to enormous cacti, to the twisted symmetry of the Monterey cypress, whose wind-contorted shapes can be seen haunting the coast above and below the city of its naming and whose delicate grace resembles the serene lines of a nineteenth-century Japanese landscape. The names of California's trees suggest the panoply that still covers a great expanse of her plains and hills, deserts and mountains: the yucca tree, the California buckeye, manzanita, broad-leafed maple, madrona, the California laurel, yellow pine, Douglas fir, incense cedar, mountain birch, white oak, scrub oak, the Fremont cottonwood, golden oak, black oak, Jeffrey pine, lodgepole pine, sugar pine, silver pine, foxtail pine—trees that represent a full spectrum of botanical life, from the lowest river bottom to the high edge of timberline.

The greatest of them all, of course, are the two redwoods, the magnificent breed that has for more than a century inspired men to poetry more often sonorous than sensible. The coast Redwood, *Sequoia sempervirens*, inhabits the Coast Range from the Santa Lucia mountains to the Oregon state line, but reaches its most impressive proportions in the expansive forests of the north. With trunks as much as fifteen to twenty-five feet in diameter, the coast redwood commonly grows to more than three hundred feet in height, and the National Geographic Society recently discovered one that measured 367.8 feet—which would seem to qualify it as the world's tallest living thing. The "big tree", *Sequoia gigantea*, unlike the coast redwood, does not exist in belts of continuous forests but in about 35 isolated groves, scattered from the American River to the Tule; some of the most impressive groves are preserved in Sequoia National Park. The coast redwoods may be the world's tallest living things, but the thicker, sturdier *Sequoia gigantea* are unquestionably some of the world's oldest living things; tree-ring counts have indicated that many are as much as 4,000 years of age. The seedlings of such trees would have broken ground long before the Athenian Empire, before Aristotle, Pericles, and Socrates—before the first flowering of man's mind. It is well not to shout unless absolutely necessary when standing in a grove of such trees.

Wilderness lovers from John Muir to Stewart Udall have proselytized for the protection of the redwood from the incursions of loggers, who long ago stripped much of the coast redwoods from the ranges south of San Francisco. The great size of the trees (which can be measured in astonishing numbers of board-feet), together with the exceptional durability of their wood, has made them a prime factor in California's timber industry. But to cut down a redwood is not to cut down a tree; it is to abort history, to end a period of living time. This last year, Congress finally passed a bill creating a Redwood National Park north of San Francisco, and some of the greatest redwood forests will remain untouched by the meddling hand of man. The effort, even though it fell short of what some conservationist organizations wanted, should be applauded; these trees exist nowhere else on the face of the earth, and if any living thing ever needed protection by man from man, it is the California redwood.

It may also need love, but it is difficult to hug a redwood tree.

3

California's interior topography, as so briefly outlined in the preceding section, provides more than enough for any man in search of a California to call his own. For myself, I will take the coast, for it is here that I feel most at home; it is here that the essence of the state's beauty catches me; it is here, where the elements of wind and sea still carry a hint of the power to destroy man and all his works, that I have found the most of my many Californias.

The fondness is natural enough. I was reared less than sixty miles from the south coast, and my parents were inordinately fond of the sea. It was still an age when the weekend automobile excursion was as much a part of family life as Fibber McGee and Molly (and perhaps the last age in which such excursions could even remotely be described as pleasurable); with a carload of brothers and sisters, cardboard cartons of food, frequently the family dog, and my parents, we would rattle down the narrow highway between San Bernardino and the coast, a pleasant, leisurely drive before the era of freeways, until we reached our destination, which was usually Doheny Beach, Newport Beach, or San Clemente. We would return late in the afternoon, sun- and water-beaten, hot, irritable—and looking forward to the next trip. To these summer-time excursions were added vacation weeks in tents, living in a grandly primitive state, learning to endure sand in our food and fleas in our sleeping bags, turning as brown as basted chickens.

I learned to use a surfboard, badly, to be sure, in the days before it became a mainstay of pop culture; I learned to skin-dive in the days before most kids could afford the incredible scuba equipment that has transformed an impromptu sport into a complicated avocation for thrill-seeking weekenders—when I went fishing for abalone, it was with a tire iron and a fishing mask. I swam like a demented child, letting the great surf of the south coast batter me mindless for hour after hour in an ecstacy of physical vigor. I climbed cliffs, explored sea-caves, searched tide pools for hermit crabs and sea anemones, dug after the squirming little sand dabs that the surf brought crashing in to burrow frantically out of sight, walked great empty miles of beach in search of shells and stones shined by the sea, and sat on the sand in the late afternoon, alone, wondering over the beginning and the end of things. I suppose freedom can be called many things, but the period of my life in which the south coast punctuated my days was as close to pure freedom as I will ever get.

All that is gone, now, gone for more than ten years. The great crescent of coast between San Diego and Long Beach has long ago succumbed to the sleek plastic and neon amenities of twentieth-century civilization. Freeways crowd the coast; you can now get from San Bernardino to Newport Beach in a little over forty-five minutes, if you push it. How can a day be an adventure if you need only forty-five minutes to find it? Motels, trailer courts, resorts, restaurants, housing developments, drive-in theatres—the coast is infested with them. Newport Beach and San Clemente, once sleepy little fishing and recreation towns, have become Miami Beaches, Doheny State Park is going to get a breakwater for a marina, and Dana Point, that magnificent 300-feet cliff that I once climbed as a child, is in danger of having its top shaved off for some ghastly cheapjack development. There are waiting lists for entry to the beaches and parks, and any given summer day will find so many people crammed onto the sand and into the surf that the whole scene has the appearance of spillover from one more urban riot.

The south coast of my youth is gone the way of the dodo, but there is plenty of coastline left in California, and places yet where that elusive aura of freedom can still be captured momentarily, places whose beauty surpasses even that of a Dana Point uncluttered by the trappings of man. The best way to find it is to brave Highway One from Morro Bay to Monterey, a 100-mile trip in which sight of the sea is rarely lost for more than a moment, and where the twentieth century has been singularly unsuccessful in altering a beauty so timeless that it takes a jar of the memory to recall that civilized man has been here for more than two centuries. From Morro Bay to the Monterey County line, the road runs on a level very close to that of the sea, so close that the steady wind that blows across this wrinkled table-top land carries the smell of it and the sound of it. At the Monterey line, the road starts to climb up the western face of a portion of the Coast Range that comprises Los Padres National Forest. From this point on, the road is a twisting adventure carved into the face of antedeluvian hills; hundreds of feet below, the crashing surf traces spiderweb patterns on the sand. If you stop the car at some convenient overlook and stand at the edge to listen, you can hear the faint, gray crashing of the sea over the sound of the wind, as if you were hearing it through one of those mythical sea shells that are said to have captured for all time the sound of surf. This is the Big Sur coast, no place for the fainthearted, but just possibly the most beautiful piece of coastline anywhere on earth, and one so thoroughly formidable in its assertion of the power of wind and sea that it may never be destroyed by man.

At Monterey, and from there north to San Francisco—with such notable exceptions as a long stretch of San Mateo County—the coast again takes on the trappings of the twentieth century, although not to a degree to match that of the south coast. Above San Francisco, the land and the sea take over once again, from Point Reyes north past Cape Mendocino. Much of the beauty of this part of the coast is of a New England quality— bleak, mist-ridden, hard—and the few towns that dot the coastline here along Highway One have a white-clapboard, New England look to them, as if their founders were State-of-Mainers looking for a duplicate of their homeland. Many of them, in point of fact, were. Unlike the Big Sur coast, the north coast is comparatively rich in history, as well as beauty. Fort Ross near the mouth of the Russian River was the southernmost outpost of Russian empire on the coast of North America in the nineteenth century, and treacherous little doghole ports scattered all along the coast once were shipping points for lumber from the forests that come down to the edge of the sea. This coast, however, lacks the warmth of welcome of Big Sur which, for all its ponderous cliffs and rocky beaches, is still a place where a man can wallow in the delights of sun, sand, and surf; on the north coast a man can more profitably reflect upon his inadequacies and let his mind be washed clean by the harshness of the natural order of things. This, too, must be a kind of freedom.

4

Bayard Taylor, reporter, poet, novelist, and a seeker after adventure, came to California during the first months of the cataclysmic gold rush and became thoroughly captivated by what he saw. Upon his return to the east, he set it all down in *Eldorado, or Adventures in the Path of Empire*, one of the best accounts we have of the westward journey through the Isthmus of Panama, of San Francisco's embryonic growth, of mines and miners. He was captivated, as well, by the expanse of California, by her variety, her beauty, her seeming imperviousness to the workings of man, and he articulated in poetry a theme that has run like a life-line through the narrative of California's history:

> How art thou conquered, tamed in all the pride
>   Of savage beauty still!
> How brought, O panther of the splendid hide,
>   To know thy master's will!

Taming the state, in all her savage beauty, has been one of man's principal pre-occupations for more than a century. He has succeeded to an alarming degree. He has dammed the rivers of the north and hauled their waters to the thirsty megalopolis south of the Techachapis. He has all but denuded the once timber-rich eastern slopes of the Sierras to provide lumber for the mines of Nevada, when that state was little more than a colony of the "Wall Street of the West"—San Francisco's Montgomery Street. He washed away entire hillsides with his hydraulic mining, filling the Sacramento with silt and sludge to such an extent that hydraulic mining finally had to be outlawed. He put the great bulk of her valleys to the mechanized plow, and made the desert of the Imperial Valley "blossom as the rose". He took a shallow mud flat called the Bahia de San Pedro and with the exercise of muscle, money and technology converted it into Los Angeles Harbor, the greatest port in the western United States. He filled up nearly a quarter of San Francisco Bay. He laced the plains and mountains with railroads, and later with freeways. He scattered the land with billboards. He brought the automobile and smog to Yosemite Valley. There is very damned little he hasn't managed to do to make the state know its master's will.

In spite of the fact that technology has for more than a century been allowed to do whatever it felt was necessary for the betterment of California's citizens, the state has managed to retain much of her original impact of landscape, as I have tried to show. It is still possible to fly from Los Angeles to San Francisco and look out upon a land whose vastness would appear to have been barely touched by man's folly. There are still deserts, mountains, and coastline—there are still solitude, beauty, and wilderness. It would be easy to forget, for a moment, the fact that the final essence of California must by the nature of things be in her people—and her people are in the cities.

California is, and has always been, an urban state. She has no rural traditions to speak of. From 1850, when the vast majority of her people lived in the teeming brick, board, and shanty metropolis of San Francisco, to 1969, when more than half the population resides in Greater Los Angeles, she has been a state totally dominated by her cities. Today, more than two-thirds of the population lives either in the San Francisco area or in the Los Angeles area, and as a final consideration in attempting to understand California, it would be well to take a brief look at the two. Much has been said of the traditional "rivalry" between San Francisco and Los Angeles. In many respects, this contention is too self-conscious to be real, like the annual CAL-UCLA football game. Yet there are both physical and emotional differences between the two that are distinct and recognizable and which have contributed measurably to the cultural web of California's life.

San Francisco is California's Rome, for the first fifty years of the state's history her center of economics, society, culture, and style, and for the last seventy years a fallen empire city done in by the vigorous hordes to the south, but retaining withal her sense of style, her superb provincialism, her conviction that the glories of a lurid, if dead, past are worth more than the shadows of an uncertain future. She is cosmopolitan, tolerant, prone to perhaps fewer of the emotional agonies that have beset America in recent years than any city in the country. She is blessed by a topographic setting and a unique sense of architectural tradition that have made her one of the world's most beautiful cities. She is surrounded on all sides by the sea, which has provided her with an air of romance, perhaps spurious, that she has never gone out of the way to avoid. She is a source of enormous pride to most of the nearly four million people who live in the sphere of her influence.

Physically, Los Angeles cannot by any stretch of the imagination be called beautiful—big, yes, as sprawling as a young giant, yes, impressive, yes—but never beautiful. Constantly tearing down and building up, forever changing, the city has achieved no architecture beyond the standard antiseptic styles enforced by a monumental use of glass and concrete construction. Nor does the dry, flat plain of her setting provide beauty. An enormous cauldron of people on the make, Los Angeles has had little time for history, for looking back, for taking anything for granted; whereas most San Franciscans, at least in a piecemeal fashion, have some knowledge of the history of their city, most Angelenos do not, nor do they care particularly. Tomorrow is waiting, so who has time for yesterday? James Bryce described the mood of the West of 1889 in *The American Commonwealth,* and his words have an uncanny ring of aptness for today's Los Angeles: "This constant reaching forward to and grasping at the future does not so much express itself in words . . . as in the air of ceaseless haste and stress which prevades the West. They remind you of the crowd which Vathek found in the hall of Eblis, each darting hither and thither with swift steps and unquiet mein, driven to and fro by a fire in the heart. Time seems too short for what they have to do, and result always to come short of their desire. . . ."

Despite the fact that she lacks what the San Franciscophile would call style and beauty, and in spite of the fact that she has little sense of history, Los Angeles is one of the most exciting cities in America—perhaps the most exciting. She may well be the last frontier city in American history, for the rootless, conglomerate population she possesses is in a long tradition, as is the "reaching forward to and grasping at the future" that is the hallmark of her emotional climate today. If the final essence of California can be found in her people, it is not difficult to maintain that that essence is more accurately expressed by the vigor and futurism of Los Angeles than by the casual and somewhat retarded enterprise of San Francisco. We can lament her sprawling ugliness, her lack of focus, her ghastly megalopolitan problems, her sometimes brutal lack of taste, but to deny her the prime place in California's future, for good or ill, would be to deny history. "There is a conviction in Southern California," novelist James M. Cain once wrote, "that some sort of destiny awaits the place".

Destiny is right around the corner, waiting for the new California.

THE PLATES

THE MASONRY OF A CYCLOPS: MOUNT SAN JACINTO

California as a land of topographic extremes is given spectacular testimony by this view of Mount San Jacinto, which rises 10,800 feet from the desert floor near Palm Springs like the masonry of a cyclops. "Breathtaking" is a pallid description of its impact, and "awesome" a hopelessly inadequate word, for there is no way to convey the sheer *bigness* of this enormous chunk of rock. The delicate blossoms of the otherwise redoubtable-looking yucca plant in the foreground provide a dash of color against the gray-blue mountain backdrop—a contrast between subtlety and brute drama that is not at all uncommon in the deserts of Southern California. San Jacinto is situated on the southern side of San Gorgonio Pass, through which occasional eastward-blowing winds called *santa anas* are funnelled into the San Bernardino Valley and the Los Angeles Basin. Like the *mistrals* of Southern France, these *santa anas* have the withering properties of a breath out of hell; when they course through megalopolis, tempers flare, marriages disintegrate, and the incidence of homicide takes on alarming proportions—perhaps comforting reminders that man in all his blinding technological competence is still a creature susceptible to forces he just barely understands.

THE DEVIL'S GOLF COURSE, DEATH VALLEY

Death Valley is the essential desert. Here, time, weather, and geology have conspired to produce a landscape of the grotesque, a sometimes ghastly affront to the imagination whose various features were long ago named in a feeble effort to put the indescribable into words—the Devil's Cornfield, Furnace Creek, the Funeral Mountains, Hell's Gate, the Gnome's Workshop, Dante's View, and so on. The stygian quality of the names is more than an early exercise in black humor—it is a tacit acknowledgment that Death Valley speaks of a past that preceded human existence and of a future that will follow it; time is the only proprietor of Death Valley. One of the least hospitable areas of the Valley is the Devil's Golf Course, shown here looking west to the Panamint Range. The salt beds that cover much of the southern half of the Valley are in this area wrinkled into eerie ridges and pinnacles of saline crystals punctuated by such bitter little salt pools as that shown in the foreground. Such a wildernes would have challenged the endurance of a Moses, for all the fact that he could make drinking water by striking stones with a stick.

THE IMPROBABLE JOSHUA

If Ray Bradbury, Isacc Azimov, or any other writer of unadulterated fantasy were ever required to sit down and construct a plant from the resources of his imagination, he could hardly come up with a more outlandish vegetable than the Joshua tree, seen here in the midst of a Mojave Desert springtime. Surely, this spike-bloomed, awkward-limbed example of botanic architecture would be more appropriate gracing the ethereal landscape of some planet circling a sun on the farthest edge of the galaxy. Nevertheless, it is an earthly product, although confined for the most part to the southern portions of the Mojave 'Desert, where thousands of the trees have been preserved, orchard-like, in Joshua Tree National Monument—certainly one of the most remarkable forests on the face of the earth. The lowly creosote bush, much less impressive than the tree for which it provides a setting, is in its own way equally remarkable: it comprises the ground cover for more than seventy per cent of the Mojave Desert, an area larger than many American states and some European countries. That adds up to a lot of creosote bush.

FREEWAY SKYLINE, SAN DIEGO

Many of the earth's now-vanished civilizations erected structures more durable than the societies that built them. The Druids, for example, left us Stonehenge, and the Egyptians the Pyramids and the Sphinx; the Mayas of Central America left behind their great terraced temples and the Pueblos of the American Southwest cities made of earth. The mute bulk of such architectural leftovers provides a key to understanding times and people long gone, for the structures that survive tend to be those that eloquently summarize what was most important to a society. We're still doing it; the civilization of New York City has raised a skyline that represents the incredible thrust of its financial empire and the civilization of Southern California has made freeways to lie upon the land like lattice-work crust on a pie—a concretized example of a society's definition of itself, for Southern California is a civilization upon wheels. It is fitting, then—and somewhat ironic—that this view of the downtown skyline of San Diego, the oldest non-Indian settlement in California, is across a vista of freeways, for what has happened to San Diego over the past two centuries has happened to all of Southern California. In this temperate and once-bucolic region, where gentle padres called the Indians in from the fields with bells and the ox-drawn *carreta* was the chief vehicle, America's seventy-year love affair with the automobile has become a full-blown orgy. In Southern California there is very nearly one automobile for every two human beings, and to accommodate the flow of this particular population explosion, enough freeway concrete has been poured to pave the state of Rhode Island. Rhode Island would object; Southern California loves it.

THE CAULDRON OF LIGHT, LOS ANGELES

Seen in the harsh and too often smog-ridden light of day, the great sprawl of
Los Angeles is one of the least beautiful mosaics imaginable. Night can make a
difference, for Los Angeles is a city of lights—lights of every color conceivable,
lights that are stationary, lights that move rythmically or jerkily, house lights,
street lights, headlights, commercial lights and private lights, lights that spell
out the names of hamburger stands and oil corporations, and lights as anony-
mous as their owners. This is a city enamored of neon, and while the affair has
tended to uglify an already homely daytime city, it has given the night scene of
Los Angeles a fascinating character; a person flying into Los Angeles Inter-
national Airport on a clear night is treated to a scene of incredible impact, for
the whole Basin from the mountains to the sea is a cauldron of light whose
energy obliterates the stars.

THE REAL TINSEL, HOLLYWOOD

Oscar Levant, a full-time cynic and a sometime piano player, once remarked that "beneath all the phoney tinsel of Hollywood lies the real tinsel". The observation, like most cynical generalizations, can be taken *cum grano salis*; nevertheless, Hollywood's inescapable air of superficial glitter speaks more eloquently for the nature of the town than any other factor. Ordinary residents of Hollywood will point out—a little belligerantly—that it is not all superstars and make-believe; it houses service-station attendants, accountants, barbers, lawyers, teachers, and plumbers, just like any other community. The statement is true, but irrelevant; Hollywood is a self-constructed state of mind, a city of and in the imagination, a place where glitter and dreams are more real than service stations, an enormous factory whose products sometimes are called art —and sometimes trash. This view of the Universal City Studio lot, with its carefully made non-buildings, is a symbol for all of Hollywood; and it would be easier to be contemptuous of a city devoted to fabrications if the so-called real world were not rapidly taking on the outlines of make-believe, as a glance at the front page of any morning newspaper will illustrate. So who is to say, finally, that Hollywood's tinsel is any less real than the fantasy we're all living?

AN OVERVIEW OF THE METROPOLIS OF FANTASY

Make-believe, it should be pointed out, is big business—very big business. The bustling metropolis shown here, eventually lost in the arms of Greater Los Angeles, is the child of movie-making and, more recently, that electrical marvel known as television. Although the days have long passed when the great Hollywood studios were run like celluloid satrapies and the industry was one of the three or four largest in the state, fantasizing for fun and profit remains one of the mainstays of California's economic life, employing thousands and awarding some of its more successful minions salaries that would challenge the *largesse* of a drunken Shah. A somewhat more delicate fantasy than Hollywood is normally associated with is seen in the center foreground of the pcture; these are the Japanese Gardens, built and decorated at a cost of more than two million dollars by Adolph and Eugene Bernheimer in 1913—an age when Hollywood was still a soporific residential suburb whose inhabitants could view with amused disdain the antics of those crazy film-makers.

A LEGACY FROM DISNEY

In a world threatening to sink under the weight of its more sordid possibilities there is something peculiarly reassuring about Disneyland—the most ambitious playground in the whole world. Its purpose is as uncomplicated as were the moral principles of its founder, Walt Disney: it is dedicated solely and enthusiastically to Good Clean Fun and the making of money, and what could be a happier combination? Disney, never a darling of the intellectuals, was nevertheless a master of fantasy in a business devoted to it, and his $17,000,000 legacy in a former Anaheim orange grove is a rollickingly successful celebration of his own view of what constituted enjoyment. Ranging in its attractions from the world of purest fancy to such carefully-recreated bits of the American past as the steamboat *Mark Twain*, seen here cruising along an imitation Mississippi River, Disneyland is every child's dream of the perfect amusement park; adults should be prepared for sore feet, incredible crowds, large expenses, and—if they can shed intellectual pretensions—one hell of a good time.

LOS ANGELES COUNTY MUSEUM OF ART

Constantly building, changing, moving itself about, Los Angeles has had little time or energy to waste on developing an architecture of grace or style; an accelerated society is too busy building to build beautifully. Yet this city has erected one of the most magnificent buildings ever achieved by any civilization anywhere at any time: the Los Angeles County Museum of Art, constructed in 1965 at a cost of more than eleven million dollars. Situated on a raised plaza 600 feet in length, the museum is comprised of three buildings, or pavilions (the central pavilion, the Ahmanson Gallery, is shown here) surrounded by patios, pools, fountains, and trees. They house collections ranging from the decorative arts of Persia to the more indecipherable works of modern abstractionists, yet the museum is itself perhaps the most triumphant work of art anyone could care to see—an island of truly timeless beauty situated smack in the center of Wilshire Boulevard's hodge-podge Miracle Mile.

A MEGALOPOLITAN PARADOX, LOS ANGELES CIVIC CENTER

If anyone should doubt that Los Angeles is a city almost totally devoted to futurism and the nebulous but tantalizing hopes it offers to those properly attuned, he need only contemplate the great, unplanned metropolis that has oozed into nearly every corner of the Los Angeles Basin, uncontrolled, over-developed, largely disorganized, and poorly governed. It is a city energized by dreams that some will say are no more than nightmares in disguise. A more comforting indication of that same futurism is the new Civic Center complex, shown here in a night scene looking toward the Dorothy Chandler Pavilion of the Music Center for the Performing Arts. The Pavilion, a symphony hall and opera house capable of seating more than three thousand people, was completed in December of 1964 as the principal feature of the Music Center, which includes a major auditorium and a theatre-in-the-round. The same energy that has produced megalopolis has also put together this stunning exercise in enlightened municipal development—one more of about ten thousand paradoxes typical of California in this, the last third of the twentieth century.

THE DEFINITIVE MISSION

The question of which is the most beautiful of California's surviving missions is one to be avoided by the prudent. Among mission-lovers it is a point of no little contention, as discussions regarding the relative talents of Sandy Koufax and Grover Cleveland Alexander are likely to be among baseball nuts. Nevertheless, as prudent as I am, I would have to vote for Mission San Carlos Borromeo, situated on the cypress-covered slopes above Carmel Bay just south of the Monterey Peninsula—a natural setting almost perfectly suited to the muted grace of the mission buildings. This was the second mission in California, founded at Monterey in 1770 by Junipero Serra, who moved it to Carmel Bay the following year in order to remove his impressionable Indian charges from the influence of debauching Spanish soldiers; it was a reasonable thing to do, for historians estimate that during the years of Spanish and Mexican rule at least five thousand California Indians died from venereal disease, one of the more virulent imports of European civilization. The Yankees, being impatient types, didn't wait around for disease to do the job. They simply and systematically set out to eliminate the natives, until by the end of the nineteenth century there were less than thirty thousand left out of an estimated population of 133,000. The history books do not call this genocide.

A HOME FOR THE SWALLOWS

Mission-watching is a century-old California recreation. Among the state's more magnetic tourist attractions—San Francisco, Yosemite National Park, etc.—the missions must be ranked near the top. For some California residents, attraction becomes obsession; whole families will spend their summer vacations patiently driving from one to another of the twenty-one missions, crossing them off the list grimly, as a shopper will cross chives, rutabagas, and pork chops off a grocery list. Such people also invariably invite the neighbors in to view the summer's collection of color slides. Even for those who care nothing about the missions, however, the name of Mission San Juan Capistrano, whose crumbling remains are seen here, is familiar. The swallows are responsible (as they are responsible for at least one bad song and hundreds of trembling little poems). Every year on St. John's Day, October 25, the swallows leave the mission for their annual migration; every year on St. Joseph's Day, March 19, they return, while tourists gather to applaud. A particularly vicious rumor has it that the San Juan Capistrano Chamber of Commerce hires a truckload of trained swallows to be released just over the hill from the mission every year. This is not true.

A LEGACY FROM HEARST

Like many Great Men, the late William Randolph Hearst collected things—castles, palaces, villas, statues, paintings, tapestries, Pompeiian mosaics, swimming pools, colonnades, marble medallions, antiques, furniture from foreign monasteries, that sort of thing. Most of it found its way sooner or later to his enormous San Simeon estate south of Morro Bay on the California coast. He called it *La Cuesta Encantada*—The Enchanted Hill—and any motorist glimpsing the great Spanish castle on a hill just west of Highway One will be forced to agree with his description. After his death in 1951, the Hearst Corporation donated San Simeon to the state, which now operates it as a state historical monument. Among the estate's outstanding features is the white marble swimming pool shown here; it is said to hold 250,000 gallons of water. Another is the great castle itself, which contains 100 rooms, including 38 bedrooms, 31 bathrooms (the discrepancy is not explained), and 14 sitting rooms. Gene Fowler, one of Hearst's most famous newspaper employees, was once called to a meeting with the publisher at San Simeon. He found him in the castle's huge master bedroom. On the floor were spread editions of all the Hearst papers, from the San Francisco *Examiner* to the New York *American*. Hearst was clad in pajamas, barefoot, with a glass of milk in one hand and a cookie in the other; walking slowly from one newspaper to the other, he read them all—turning the pages with his toes. At heart, Great Men are Simple Men.

THE POET'S COAST

This is the Big Sur coast, whose wind-whipped beauty has drawn more than
two generations of poets, artists, lovers, and other refugees from a world
reluctant to make room for life. There is life here, and breath, and space to
open up all the senses. This is poet's country, and few recognized it more fully
than Robinson Jeffers, whose poetry was never far removed from the taste and
smell of salt spray. It was on this coast that he made the beautiful Tamar dance
courting the spirits of the dead: "And the sea moved, on the obscure bed of her
eternity, but both were voiceless. . . ."

GOING, GOING...

This bucolic scene, looking toward the town of Exeter on the east side of the San Joaquin Valley, is representative of a region that has done its share toward making California the leading agricultural state in the nation. The total annual value of California's agricultural product ranges between 3.5 and 4 billion dollars, produced by more than 90,000 farms of an average size of 371 acres, although many go into the multiples of thousands of acres. This is industry on a monumental scale: a good-sized farm specializing in one product or another will have a staff that includes a manager, his assistants, an office staff, a physician, an electrician, a mechanic and assistants, a cook and assistants, and a field labor force of up to 2,000 during the harvest season. It is also a disappearing industry, as hard as that may be to believe. California's rate of urbanization is so accelerated that every day 375 acres of open space (most of it agricultural land) disappears beneath a smother of blacktop, concrete, housing, and industry. In *How to Kill a Golden State*, William Bronson estimates that if the present rate of urbanization continues for another fifty years, *all* of California's agricultural land will vanish, and such scenes as this will be mainly of historical value—like the view of an orange grove in the San Fernando valley.

SEQUOIA GIGANTEA

John Muir, the spiritual father of American conservation, described the Big Trees of the southern Sierras as well as anyone ever has or ever will. He was writing in 1878: "The average stature attained by the Big Tree under favorable conditions is perhaps about 275 feet, with a diameter of twenty feet. Few full-grown specimens fall much short of this, while many are twenty-five feet in diameter and nearly 300 feet high. . . . Yet so exquisitely harmonious are even the very mightiest of these monarchs . . . there never is anything overgrown or huge-looking about them, not to say monstrous; and the first exclamation on coming upon a group for the first time is usually, 'See what *beautiful* trees!' Their real godlike grandeur . . . is invisible. . . . Even the mere arithmetical greatness is never guessed by the inexperienced as long as the tree is comprehended from a little distance in one harmonious view. When, however, we approach so near that only the lower portion of the trunk is seen, and walk round and round the wide bulging base, then we begin to wonder at their vastness. . . . Sequoias bulge considerably at the base, yet not more than is required for beauty and safety; and the only reason that this bulging is so often remarked as excessive is because so small a section of the shaft is seen at once. The real taper of the trunk, beheld as a unit, is perfectly charming in its exquisite fineness, and the appreciative eye ranges the massive columns, from the swelling, muscular instep to the lofty summit dissolving in a crown of verdure, rejoicing in the unrivaled display of giant grandeur and giant loveliness." Because of their beauty—and, the cynic is forced to note, because their wood makes much inferior lumber to that of its cousin, the *sempervirens-sequoia gigantea* has been superbly preserved in 36,000 scattered acres protecting ninety-nine per cent of all the Big Trees in existence. Muir would be pleased.

THE HYPERBOLE OF NATURE: YOSEMITE VALLEY

What does one say about the Yosemite Valley that hasn't been said ten thousand times before—and better? Attempting to embroider with words this winter scene of Glacier Point and the Merced River, for instance, would be about as utilitarian as a poet's explanation of such abstractions as heaven, hell, love, the female mind, and death. In the Yosemite Valley, nature provides its own hyperbole. In lieu of description—or even reflection—then, let me offer a few prosaic facts: The Valley was discovered by civilized man in 1851, when the "Mariposa Battalion", a collection of Yankee Indian-hunters in pursuit of a band of recalcitrant Miwoks, came upon what is now called Inspiration Point—whose view of the Valley was fully as mind-boggling to the Battalion as it is to today's motorist. In 1864, the Valley was deeded by the federal government to California for a state park; in 1890, Yosemite National Park was created, and in 1906 Yosemite State Park was absorbed by it. The park spreads over 752,744 acres and includes 429 lakes, two rivers, a chain of mountain peaks, five major waterfalls and many smaller ones, stands of Big Trees, 1,200 varieties of flowering plants and ferns, squirrels, chipmunks, deer, bear, reptiles, amphibians, and 230 varieties of birds.

THE BEAUTIFUL VICTIM

That Yosemite Valley is one of the greatest extravaganzas in the natural panoply of the world is amply illustrated by this view of Vernal and Nevada Falls as seen from Glacier Point. What is not obvious in this and most other photographs of the Valley is the fact that Yosemite is a region in desperate trouble, threatened by its own popularity, as are many of the national parks. The immediate culprit can be identified: the automobile, that technological marvel which has converted many of our cities into cauldrons of smog and our highways into scenes of random carnage. James Bryce, British Ambassador to the United States (his brilliant *American Commonwealth* has been cited in the introduction to this book) saw the problem as early as 1912: "If Adam had known what harm the serpent was going to work, he would have tried to prevent him from finding lodgment in Eden; and if you were to realize what the result of the automobile will be in that wonderful, that incomparable valley, you will keep it out." Not even the prescient Bryce could have foreseen the phenomenon of smog, but he knew what has since become altogether too obvious: the automobile was a deadly threat to the aesthetic and ecological integrity of one of the three or four most beautiful natural areas on earth. The Department of the Interior disagreed with Bryce, and in 1913 gave permission for automobiles to enter Yosemite Valley. Today, more than 500,000 automobiles enter the Valley every year. Groves and orchards and meadows have disappeared under a smear of asphalt for parking lots; traffic on a typical summer Sunday afternoon is indistinguishable from the streams of commuters in megalopolis; the sound, smell, and effluence of the internal combustion engine competes with the wonders of Half Dome twenty-four hours a day. The whole dismal spectacle seems to justify one in questioning the theory that man is a learning animal.

SQUAW VALLEY: A GOOD PLACE TO DIE

The peculiar and altogether unique tendency of the human animal to subject himself in the name of fun to potential mutilation—and even death—is represented by a number of currently popular sports, including mountain climbing, skydiving, ballooning, gliding, spelunking, and motor-cycle riding. Skiing is one of the oldest, as well as one practically guaranteed to produce any number of impressive injuries, all of which are insurable. One of the most attractive places to throw yourself into it, if it seems necessary, is Squaw Valley State Recreation Area in the Sierra Nevada, not far from Tahoe City. Situated in a splendid natural bowl at the six thousand foot level, the 1,000-acre skiing area was the site chosen for the 1960 Winter Olympics. Skiing for fun in California goes back farther than one might expect. As early as 1856, *Hutching's California Magazine* could report on the growing popularity of what it called "snowshoeing", complete with a woodcut rendering of a group of happy "snowshoers" sliding and tumbling down a Sierran slope; one of the woodcut's figures, predictably enough, appears to have broken his leg.

TAKEN BY THE WIND: BUTTE STORE, VOLCANO

A little more than a century ago, the western foothills of the Sierra Nevada were the scene of one of the most astonishing adventures in history—the California Gold Rush. This was the "Mother Lode" country, whose name was taken from the hard-dying conviction that somewhere in its hills was the greatest solid deposit of gold on earth—the ultimate source of all the loose wealth that littered the westward-flowing streams that fed into the Sacramento Valley. That deposit, geologically impossible, never was discovered, but this is still called Mother Lode country, and remnants of the once-frenetic culture it spawned can yet be seen scattered through the hills. One of them is Volcano, once among the richest and most populous towns in the Mother Lode. Founded in 1849 in a crater-like hollow rimmed by fir-covered hills, Volcano soon boasted all the paraphernalia common to the mining boom town—saloons, brothels, fandango halls, assay offices, real estate brokers, and lawyers, as well as a Thespian Society and a Miners Library Association. Today, much of Volcano is a relic, as are most of the once-flourishing boom towns of the Mother Lode—their populations diminished or gone, their streets weedgrown and deserted, and their ambitious architecture left to the vagaries of the wind.

COURTHOUSE AND CANNON: BRIDGEPORT

Bridgeport, on the eastern slopes of the Sierra Nevada, owes its existence to a mining frenzy that followed the mood and tone of the great Gold Rush—even if it never attained quite the same level of trauma or significance. Goldseekers frustrated by the lamentable paucity of loose gold in California after 1849 wandered into and over the Sierra, never quite giving up the dream. Some found an answer to the quest in western Nevada, where gold existed in varying degrees of quality and quantity, and the region entered a period of staccato excitement that lasted well into the twentieth century. One of the excitements was Aurora, a boom town of the 1860s, and one its citizens proudly considered worthy of its role as the seat of Mono County—until they discovered that Aurora was in Nevada, not California. In 1864, authorities hastily transferred all county records across the state line and set up shop in a roadside camp that later became Bridgeport. The town flourished well enough for the building of Mono County Court House, seen here, but like most towns dependent upon the fragility of a mining economy, Bridgeport steadily declined; today, its population is less than two hundred. The courthouse is still one of the region's leading tourist attractions, however, and its cannon on the front lawn gained some local repute as a favorite repository for illegal booze during Prohibition. Cannons have been put to worse uses.

THE FINITE RESOURCE: LAKE TAHOE

In *Roughing It*, Mark Twain penned an admirable tribute to Lake Tahoe: "We plodded on, and at last the lake burst upon us, a noble sheet of blue water . . . walled in by a rim of snow-clad peaks that towered aloft full 3,000 feet higher still. As it lay there with the shadows of the mountains brilliantly photographed upon its still surface, I thought it must surely be the fairest picture the whole earth affords." Few today would disagree with him; airline pilots interrupt first-run movies to point out this shimmering gem of a lake to their passengers. What the passengers can't see, and what too many others ignore even when they *can* see it, is the slot-machine culture that has encrusted the forested beauty of the lake-shore with some of the most appallingly crude examples of ticky-tacky in existence. Even more ominous is what this same culture has done and continues to do to the lake itself. Effluents from casinos, high-rise condominiums, motels, hotels, houses, cabins, and service-station restrooms have for years been dumped into the lake indiscriminately. If it is allowed to continue, Tahoe will be reduced to a condition approaching the sterile gray-green sludge of Lake Erie, since become a national disgrace. And it continues. Natural beauty is a finite resource, and nowhere is its fragility more apparent or pathetic than in the Tahoe Basin, where time is running out for the "jewel of the Sierra".

SAN FRANCISCO SKYLINE

At least one critic has called it a "Disneyland for intellectuals", and it is true that San Francisco possesses a kind of flashy, carnival, amusement-center appeal that can be mistaken for the real thing. From the rarified delights of the topless-bottomless-totally-naked emporiums of Broadway's tawdry strip to family fun aboard a clattering, magnificently overloaded cable car, the city is a cornucopia for tourists, who come every year by the hundreds and hundreds of thousands—driving the wrong way on one-way streets, nearly being run over by Muni buses, being touched for nickels, dimes, and quarters by Howard Street hobos and Haight Street hippies, getting lost in North Beach, freezing in summer and sweltering in winter, having their cars towed away from tow-away zones, buying oddball curios in Chinatown shops, wandering unawares into gay bars, getting stoned at the Top-of-the-Mark, being skinned alive in bars serving watered-down drinks at outrageous prices in exchange for the dubious privilege of watching some swinger phlegmatically gyrate her naked breasts, and loving every hectoring minute of it. Beneath all this chamber of commerce patina, however, lies one of the few cities in America that still possesses the mood, tone and quality called style—a combination of quiet cynicism, physical beauty, a kind of reverence for human oddities, splendid provincialism, and an affection for the details of a sometimes lurid past that is reflected in the city's architecture, or that portion of it that has managed to escape the onslaught of such unbelievable monoliths as the Bank of America's World Headquarters Building, seen here under construction but already dominating the cityscape as it dominates the financial world with its assets of more than twenty billion dollars.

SUNRISE OVER THE GOLDEN GATE

"Chrysopylae", the Gate of Gold, John Charles Fremont called it in 1846, three years before the discovery of the Mother Lode's treasures sent more than 40,000 argonauts streaming into San Francisco Bay from all points of the compass. The name stuck, for obvious reasons. Spanned now by the massive delicacy of the red-orange bridge, the Golden Gate is still one of the most dramatic port entrances in all the world—a drama frequently abetted in stupendous fashion by a cooperative nature, as in this view: a new day and perhaps a new promise. Who could enter the Golden Gate and not feel the assurance expressed in the salutation Jessie and John Fremont used in their letters to each other—"*Les Bons Temps Viendra*"—the good times will come?

MOONRISE OVER SAN FRANCISCO

"I'd rather be a busted lamp-post on Battery Street than the Waldorf-Astoria", one of San Francisco's more articulate pugilists is believed to have remarked a long time ago. The observation has long since taken a favorite place in the city's lexicon of self-admiration—San Franciscans are superbly adept at quoting San Franciscans on the delights of San Francisco. Nights like the one shown here give one to sympathize with the affection that fostered the remark, for it is not possible to live in a city that can assault you with such glimmering beauty without responding to it. Moments like this stun the mind, allowing you to forget days of smog, hopeless traffic, the Embarcadero Freeway, Chinatown gangs, your latest hangover, the city administration, and the Bank of America's Headquarters Building.

THE LAST OF THE FLOWER DRUM SONG

The neon-ridden, penny-arcade facade of San Francisco's Chinatown has been a picture-postcard mainstay for more than two generations, and there is much to be said for the flash of color it gives the city and the tourist dollars it brings in. It contains some of the best restaurants in the United States and any number of shops offering exquisitely-contrived items imported from all over the eastern world. Chinatown is also one of the worst metropolitan slums in California. The 1960 census listed some 36,000 Chinese in San Francisco, most of them clustered in and about the environs of Chinatown, and the number has grown since then. They are inadequately housed, ill-fed, and incredibly poor. "Sweat shop" is a term that originated on New York City's East Side, but it might as well have been born in Chinatown; one of the enclave's less-publicized features is the existence of garment shops where women sew for ten or twelve hours a day at wages that would appall a Mississippi cotton-picker. The men do little better. So, while the city pretends that nothing is wrong, while the Six Companies—the "City Hall" of Chinatown—makes vague pronouncements about as effective or relevant as a Junior League charity drive, and while the tourists come to gape and buy, gangs of youthful Chinese patterning themselves after black militants have taken to the streets. It is all a long way from the days of *The Flower Drum Song*.

A BATTERING-RAM FOR MONTGOMERY STREET

This unusual pedestrian's eye-view of the San Francisco skyline sums up much of the city's recent architectural history: the good old buildings are giving way to glass-and-concrete testimonials to corporate vigor, epitomized here by the forty-three-story Wells, Fargo Bank Building plunging into the heart of Montgomery Street like a fiscal battering-ram. The city is changing, particularly in the downtown area, changing so fast that a bookstore you browse in during one month might be wiped out the next, to be replaced by a multi-level parking lot or one more skycraper. One can—one does—lament the gradual destruction of an architecture admirably suited to the style of one of the world's great cities, but there seems to be little that anyone can do to stop it; not even the some-times rakish noncomformity of San Francisco can apparently withstand the juggernaut of Progress and Enterprise.

SEQUOIA SEMPERVIRENS

The coast redwood, unlike *sequoia gigantea*, has from its discovery by man been an uncommonly popular timber resource. The Indians, lacking the necessary technology for cutting them down, utilized deadfalls; the Spanish cut them down very nicely, however, as did the Mexicans and later the ingenius Yankees, who disposed of more redwood trees in twenty years than all the cultures that preceded them. By 1900, the bulk of the stands that once stretched nearly unbroken from Santa Barbara to San Francisco were largely depleted. Those of the North Coast were not, however, and since that time most of the redwood timber industry has functioned in this region. The potential returns have been impressive. In 1965, for example, the total income *after taxes* of the Arcata Redwood Company (one of the largest) was $2,639,472. It is understandable, then, that when conservationists began a serious drive for the creation of a Redwood National Park in the 1960s, the lumber industry fought the concept tooth and claw. Led by the determined Sierra Club and supported by a growing national awareness that these were, indeed, the "last redwoods", the conservationists finally overcame frustration, opposition, dissension, antagonism, and political apathy; in September, 1968, Congress passed an act creating a 58,000-acre Redwood National Park, and on October 2, President Lyndon B. Johnson signed it into law.

A LEGACY FROM THE CZAR

Situated on headlands overlooking the sea some eighty miles north of San Francisco, Fort Ross is surely one of the most remarkable of California's man-made landmarks. It was founded in 1812 by the Russian-American Fur Company as a base for sea otter and fur seal hunting and for producing food for the company's Alaskan settlements. Its construction inspired dismay in Mexico City, from which Spanish California was more-or-less governed, for fear that the Russians would expand even farther (could this be considered an early version of the domino theory?). Nothing much ever came of the situation, however, and by the time the United States began to eye California specula-tively, the Russian enterprise, never very successful, was on its last legs. In 1841, the Russians sold the land and the fort to Johann August Sutter, the founder of New Helvetia, soon to become Sacramento. Sutter's ambitions for the fort were even shorter-lived than those of the Russians, and it fell into disuse. The earth-quake of 1906 did considerable damage to the buildings; most were ultimately restored by the state, and today the whole complex is a State Historical Land-mark—complete with a small museum, formerly the governor's residence, and the oldest Russian Orthodox church (the fort's chapel, built in 1828) in the continental United States outside Alaska.

BODEGA-BY-THE-BAY

As you travel north from San Francisco on Highway One, snaking its way above the sea and across rolling hills that resemble nothing so much as the moors of England, one of the dividends is the number of small towns tucked into nooks and crannies of the landscape. Dependent upon agriculture, the sea, and a sporadic tourist trade for their existence, most of these towns have remained generally uncluttered by the most offensive detritus of the twentieth century (the North Coast, for example, does not have a freeway, although the State Division of Highways would dearly love to boondoggle one through). One of the most charming of the towns is Bodega, near the shores of Bodega Bay. The harsh, sometimes stark beauty of the land is somehow emphasized by the spare, New England quality of much of the town's architecture. Shown here is the local church, and in the rear the town school, first constructed in 1856. Both buildings were featured in Alfred Hitchcock's scarifying film, *The Birds*. The schoolhouse is now operated as an art gallery showing the work of some of the many artists who have moved north to capture the wild, free appeal of a country wedded to the sea.

OPPONENTS: LAND AND SEA ON THE NORTH COAST

Much of the coast above the mouth of the Russian River has an appearance of disintegration, as if the land were steadily crumbling into the sea. Block-like headlands, angular coves, and huge, isolated chunks of land weave along the coast like the lacework edge of a linen tablecloth. Around it all is the gray crashing of a sea that is much more obviously the opponent of the land than anywhere else on the California coast. The sheer, eternal *power* of the sea becomes awesomely apparent as you stand over it on one of these headlands and watch it smashing into the continent's edge. "The tides are in our veins," Robinson Jeffers once wrote; on the North Coast you feel in your skin the pulse of all time and life.

THE OLD WHITE LADY: MOUNT SHASTA

Mt. Shasta is known as "the old White Lady of the North" to airline pilots who rely upon her as a constant point of reference. Surely the most majestic of all California peaks, 14,000-feet Mt. Shasta might also serve us here as another point of reference: a reminder that the variety and profundity of natural beauty that California yet possesses is a resource all too susceptible to the raging insensitivity of man and his screaming technology. The weight of all history has taught us that; yet if we look around us at what is happening, as I have on occasion tried to do in this book, it is possible to wonder as one writer did, whether it is true that "what we learn from history is that we learn nothing from history". We will be held accountable for the world we create. The legacy of any generation is the quality of the environment it has shaped. If California is indeed to be the new America, then Californians and all those who care for the future had better heed the words of Isaiah: "Surely your turning of things upside down shall be esteemed as the potter's clay; for shall the work say of him that made it, He made me not? or shall the thing framed say of him that framed it, He had no understanding?"